CASTLES

Christopher Chant

Published by Roydon Publishing Co. Ltd.
London
England

ISBN 0946674 418

Printed in Portugal

Produced by Talos Books Limited
Lincolnshire, Great Britain

Edited by Diane Moore
Designed by Brian Benson
Picture Research by Jonathan Moore
Phototypesetting by Swiftprint Ltd. Stamford, Lincs.

CASTLES

Christopher Chant

Perched at the head of one of the most northerly points in Northern Ireland, close to Bushmills in County Antrim, Dunluce Castle was abandoned shortly after 1639, when the kitchen and its occupants slid off the cliff into the sea.

CASTLES OF BRITAIN & IRELAND

The castle as we know it has its origins in the mediaeval ages, and reflects with peculiar emphasis the characteristics of the socio-economic and military conditions of the era. So what are today treasured relics or interesting ruins were then keys to the control of whole geographical regions. For the castle was the fortified home and headquarters of a nobleman, housing the feudal overlord of the area, his family and retainers (civil and military) together with stores of all the necessities required against siege. And it must be emphasized that whereas modern fortifications have been almost exclusively military in origin and content, the mediaeval castle was a joint civil and military undertaking, a fortified geographical feature wherein of the feudal lord and his administration could shut themselves up under the protection of personally loyal troops and so dominate his territorial holdings. In time of peace the castle was in effect a walled village or small town, the capital of the area and the centre of the judicial and financial systems, while in time of war the gates could be closed in the event of an enemy's investing the castle, And as long as the castle held out, the invader had little or no chance of consolidating his hold on the desired area.

Yet though this type of castle reached its apogee in the mediaeval era, its origins stretch back to the dawn of civilization, when small communes sought to protect themselves and their flocks against marauders in massive earthworks now known as Iron Age forts. Classic examples in the United Kingdom are Maiden Castle, Old Sarum and the like, whose massive earth ramparts and ditches are a puissant reminder of the capabilities of these technologically poor peoples. It should be noted, however, that such Iron Age forts were communal undertakings, and not the possessions of a single lord. And the same may be said of the succeeding types of fortification built in northern Europe by the Celts, Saxons, Viking and Germanic tribes: these were essentially communities acting for their own defence and security. There were also purely military fortifications, the most notable being the Romans' fortified camps and castles, but these were primarily of military value, and it was not until the Middle Ages that the classic castle, the sign of a true feudal lord, began to appear as a complement to the fortified community. The two flourished together, it must be noted, and the feudal lord often built his castle within the boundaries of a fortified town, good examples being the Tower of London within the walled urban community.

The castle also reflected the military technology of its day, which lacked explosives and aircraft. It was thus planned as a refuge and base against armies comprising foot soldiers, a small amount of cavalry and a relatively minute engineering capability. In realistic terms the castle was relatively immune to all but surprise attack and prolonged siege: the former

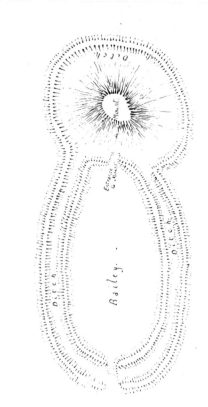

Early Norman castles, such as that at Trecastle in Brecknock, were of the simple motte-and-bailey type, the vital motte being protected by its own ditched defences and an outer ditched bailey.

was always a possibility, and could only be guarded against by the use of patrols and good intelligence of neighbours' intentions; the latter presented different problems, but careful lords maintained adequate stocks of food for people and animals, and built their castles over a plentiful supply of running water. Sieges rarely lasted more than a few months, the attacking forces having to return most of their troops home by the late summer for the harvest, and this factor was used as a yardstick for supply holdings.

As a factor linked intricately with feudalism, the castle as an architectural type spread with feudalism, starting in the Loire valley in France (about 950 AD) and spreading rapidly to the rest of northern France; the next steps were into the Rhineland and central, then southern, France; then followed western Germany, Germany proper and England after 1066; and finally the expansion of the Normans and their descendants took castle building to Scotland, Wales and Ireland, to southern Italy and Sicily, to the Peloponese, and to the near Middle East. A comparable expansion took place in the Iberian peninsula as the Moors were slowly driven out, the Spaniards and Portuguese consolidating

Core of the Norman defences in London was the Tower of London, started by William I. The White Tower is the defensive centrepiece of this imposing monument.

their newly-expanding feudalism with a large number of castles. It is often ill appreciated how prolific a race of castle-builders the Normans were: in England (including Monmouthshire), for example, the Normans built castles on at least 1,223 sites, with another 367 in Wales. These were not, of course, all vast edifices like the Tower of London, but rather a mixed bag of castles large and small as suited to the particular needs of administering and keeping subservient the populations of any given feudal holding seized by the Normans during their conquest of the country. Major administrative centres with powerful garrisons had inevitably to be built at strategic locations where communications, terrain and water were suitable, but these were often supported (or replaced in less hospitable regions) by smaller castles designed more for tactical than strategic considerations. The Normans were thus able to construct a network of castles small and large that served to ensure the tactical and strategic domination of a Norman aristocracy in a Saxon land.

Any understanding of the connotations of the term 'castle' must inevitably centre on the nature of the society that built them, and the Normans who originated the type were epitomes of a military society in which all virtues were subject to the overriding imperative of military security and capability. The Normans grew powerful as a military force without contemporary comparison, and never lost sight of this fact. They realized that their numbers were small, and that continued dominance was therefore centred on qualitative superiority. So the Normans could not spread themselves thinly over their lands, but must exist in small concentrations secure from surprise attack and overwhelming. But it must not be imagined that castles were consequently purely defensive structures: the castle was indeed a refuge, wherein the lord and his troops could rest assured that they were all but immune from surprise attack, but it was also a base for offensive operations within the geographical area. The network of Norman castles in England meant that there were few places that lay more than a few hours march from a castle. And as the Normans pushed forward to the dominance of new areas, their castles acted as forward bases for the offensive, offering secure points on their lines of communication and choke points for any enemy activite during the winter months. To this extent, therefore, the Norman castle was a centre of offense as well as defence: the great castles of the Welsh marches, such as Ludlow and Chester, did indeed prevent or help prevent Welsh incursions into England, but also paved the way for operations into Wales. And as Wales fell to the Norman onslaught, the march castles ceased to have a primary function, their place being taken by newer castles such as Conway and Harlech within the country and by

Left: Rhuddlan was one of the most important Welsh castles of Edward I's scheme, and is still a most impressive site providing ample evidence of the castle's monumental strength.
Below: Dominating the town and the crossing of the River Teme in Shropshire, Ludlow Castle was a pivot of the Welsh Marches' defences, and is still in good condition.

Flint and Rhuddlan dominating the approaches to these fortresses. The castle combined the functions of fortress and residence, as noted above, and though the former role was always dominant given the nature of the Normans' military society, the latter was nevertheless important. Consciously or unconsciously, the Normans and their legatees realized that military dominance of terrain had to be accompanied by social and economic influences if the region were to be truly pacified and brought into the Norman way of life. And though the feudal way of life may today seem stratified into a number of strictly differentiated classes, this was most certainly not the case, for in real terms there were only two classes: the feudal lord and his household, and the servants. The lord's household was itself large, and comprised the lord's family and friends, plus all who had sworn fealty to him, notably lesser nobles and military leaders, though the two 'sub-classes' cannot really be split in an essentially military society. In the widest possible sense, therefore, the household was the lord's family, which goes far to explaining the fact that mediaeval castles did not have separate barracks for the troops or quarters for the servants: these were both classed as being outside the family, and had to make do with the hall or other areas for nocturnal accommodation. In terms of living space the castle was designed almost exclusively for the household, with servants and soldiers occupying whatever spaces were left over. This latter varied from time to time, it being the sensible custom of the period for the feudal household to travel extensively within and without the lord's domain, an early version of the concept of 'showing the flag' to make sure that the lord's presence was felt at times all over his domain, where he would take up temporary residence in one of other of the main castle's outlying smaller castles of fortified houses.

With the lord travelled much of the administrative apparatus of the domain, though the principal castle remained the headquarters of this vital organ of local administration and tax collecting. However, one untruth that has become almost commonplace was the use of the castle as a prison: at times the castles did contain prisoners, but these were usually of fairly exalted rank and kept under 'protective custody' in considerable style. Prisoners held in castles were thus likely to be of the 'political' type, there being little place for conventional criminal prisoners until later in history, when the castle had lost its original function as the home and base of a feudal lord. This makes complete sense given the military nature of Norman society: what lord in his right mind would wish to burden himself and his residence with criminal riff-raff? These latter would merely occupy space better devoted to storage of emergency supplies, and in times of crisis would represent merely another useless mouth to feed and to guard. Moreover, the judicial system of the period was not geared towards lengthy incarceration, but rather towards the alternatives of execution or local justice in the stocks. The notion of dungeons, a corruption of the Norman *donjon* (central keep), is a later slur, dating from the period in which the castle had become redundant in its primary function but provided ample scope for the security of political prisoners and for the location of valuables such as specie and the mint.

As might be expected in a period of expansion and change, the castle itself underwent considerable change in the 400 years that were its heyday. It seems reasonable to suppose that the first castles were large earth mounds surmounted by substantial wooden structures surrounded by a wooden palisade: attacks would first have to cross the ditch made by the excavation of the mound, then scale the mound before coming face-to-face with the wooden palisade, whose defenders would meanwhile have been pelting the attackers with stones, arrows and javelins. Such earth and wood fortifications paved the way for more solidly, constructed stone castles: the early type provided the lord with solid, if short-term, protection soon after he moved into the area, and also provided the basis for the later and definitive castle. The original earth mound that raised the castle above the surrounding land and so gave the defenders improved fields of fire was usually built solidly enough to provide the footing for the later stone keep, whose stone foundations were often used as the basis for the original wood structure. Thus an overlapping construction process over a long period was possible, the wooden palisade providing protection as the wooden keep was replaced by a stone structure, and the stone keep serving as a refuge as the wooden palisade was gradually replaced by the outer walls of the castle, with towers at most angles in the wall for extra defence capability. The core of the whole arrangement was the motte (mound) topped by the donjon (keep), which was the ultimate sanctuary of the household and generally contained the household's primary accommodation. Outside the motte was the bailey, essentially a large and relatively flat expanse on which horses and troops could exercise and drill, surrounded by the curtain wall and its flanking towers, themselves protected by a large ditch or water-filled moat with clear ground beyond. The outer wall was generally designed to keep the enemy at more than missile range from the donjon, and its towers provided additional protective strongpoints as well as accommodation for the soldiers and the livestock. It is clear from the above that there were thus at least two defensive zones: outside the outer walls, where an approaching enemy could be attacked with missiles before he reached the moat, and the area inside the outer walls, where again the enemy could

Below: Controlling the coastal road in Cardigan Bay, Harlech Castle was part of Edward I's scheme for dominating North Wales, and the masterpiece of the designer, James of St. George. **Bottom:** *Conway Castle, dominating the road along the North Welsh coast, is a truly magnificent example of English castle-building capabilities.*

be checked by the defenders of the donjon if he succeeded in fighting his way past the outer defences. In larger castles the inner keep was frequently protected by its own small bailey, which surrounded the tower keep where the lord and his immediate household had their quarters.

It has often been supposed that the effective end for castles was spelled by the advent of gunpowder weapons, notably artillery. This is to a certain degree true, but disguises the fact that other factors were at work. And in the initial period after the introduction of guns, artillery emplaced in castles was more useful than the artillery used by attackers. What really marked the end for castles in their original form was a change in society, the military civilization that had built the castles being replaced slowly by a more diverse society that reflected the reduced chances of internal conflict within the countries that had built castles. With the emergence of strong kings in the 15th century, the reins of power were gathered in towards the capital, and the opportunities (and even desirability) of semi-independent feudal lords rapidly diminished as political, military and financial power were shifted towards the capital and major towns. This tendency became yet more pronounced as the efforts of early overseas explorers were turned to advantage by mercantile princes, which left the erstwhile feudal lords as masters mainly of local society. Thus the gradual demise of castle-building can be attributed to the decline of feudalism itself, which removed the primary function of the castle.

The buildings themselves, built over a period of centuries as virtually indestructible strongholds, remained in existence for the most part. Smaller castles often 'withered on the vine' and were abandoned, and others were later destroyed militarily or dismantled for their valuable stone, but the greater castles remained as the family homes of the families which had built them. These households still owned vast tracts of land, and were decisive influences in the social and economic lives of their regions, and this was reflected in the maintenance of the greater castles. But gone were the soldiers, and with their departure the outer walls were not infrequently allowed to decay. And so there remain castles aplenty all over the parts of Europe and Middle East that were once held in sway by the Norman type of feudalism: some of the castles were ruins, others are only part of what they once were, and yet others remain or have been restored to the full extent of their original power, both emotional and physical.

England abounds with castles (ruins and complete buildings) of all types, sizes and geographical locations. One of the most important of these is Arundel Castle in Sussex. Dominating the high ground in the town of the same name, Arundel Castle controls the most important reach of the river Arun, and was started soon after 1066 by Roger de Montgomery, Earl of Shrewsbury. Montgomery held the Rape of Sussex, one of the principal military districts on the southern approaches to London, and Arundel was its centrepiece. The castle has been in continuous service since its building, the Shrewsbury family replaced first by the Earls of Sussex, then the FitzAlans and finally, since the 16th century, by the Dukes of Norfolk. Some indication of the castle's importance may be gauged from the fact that its holders have always been among the noblest and most loyal in the land, as befits a castle of this importance. The present castle is from the outside little recognizable compared with the original, for the castle was extensively rebuilt according to Victorian ideas during the 19th century. The portions to suffer most in this 'restoration' were the buildings in the southern (lower) bailey, though this is still entered through the gatehouse built by Montgomery. The barbican attached to the gatehouse is 13th century. Other portions of the castle fared better in Victorian times, and the original motte survives. This latter is crowned by a 12th-century shell keep. The shell keep was often built as an alternative to the tower keep, for it was relatively cheap to build, could be added without difficulty to an existing motte and bailey stronghold, and when added to a high motte in an already commanding position offered a measure of security comparable with that of the tower keep that became a feature of later 12th-century castles. At Arundel, the original entrance to the shell keep was blocked in the 13th century and replaced by the present Well Tower. As its name suggests, the shell keep is a walled enclosure at the top of the motte, and similar keeps are to be found at Windsor, Restormel, Tamworth, Trematon, Cardiff and Carisbrooke Castles. A variant of the shell keep found at Farnham and Berkeley has the shell wall built round the lower edge of the motte, with relatively higher walls rising to the height of the top of the mound.

At the other extremity of England lies Bamburgh Castle, which like Arundel also guards the way inland, though this time from the North Sea, and also dominates the road south from Scotland. Like the castles of the Welsh marches, Bamburgh both protected England from Scots incursions across the eastern border regions, and also provided a good jumping-off point for English offensives into Scotland. The building of the castle was started soon after the Norman invasion of 1066, and was undertaken on the site of a citadel first raised by the kings of Bernicia. Bamburgh is an unusual castle in one respect, for it has no motte: given the castle's

Though still an imposing sight, Bamburgh Castle has lost much of its original 'flavour' through a series of relatively modern 'restorations'.

magnificent location on an elevation that is in itself almost impregnable, such a construction was wholly superfluous. However, Bamburgh is also notable for a fine tower keep, which was completed on the personal instruction of Henry II: the keep measures 69 ft by 61 ft, and given the commanding position of the whole castle enclosure, is a modest 55 ft high, considerably less than other good tower keeps in castles such as Dover, Castle Rising, Kenilworth and Middleham. In the case of all these structures, the term tower keep is perhaps misleading, for the keep's height is less than its linear dimensions on the ground. Bamburgh was completed in its definitive form in about 1250, but had already undergone a traumatic history, having been taken in 1095 by William Rufus from Robert de Mowbray, Earl of Northumberland. But perhaps the most important date in the castle's history was 1463, when it was taken under siege by the Earl of Warwick, the 'kingmaker'. Up to that time the castle had been considered impregnable, but with the aid of two heavy guns, named Newcastle and London,

Warwick took the castle after his success in the Battle of Hexham. Bamburgh unfortunately suffered the attentions of the Victorians, losing much of its original appearance though not configuration, and still located in the inner bailey are the King's Hall, the Captain's Hall and a large kitchen, all built in the 13th century.

Another coastal castle is Corfe in Dorset, now a ruin but for all that one of the most impressive sites (and sights) in England. By the time of the Norman conquest the site had already been occupied by a castle since at least the time of Alfred the Great, the West Saxons having seen the site as ideal for a bastion against the Danes. However, the ruins that exist today are the remains of the Purbeck stone castle founded by William the Conqueror and steadily built during the following two centuries as a magnificent, well-sited and nigh untakable wall-and-tower castle. The basic shape is like that of a banana, running from north-west to south-east. The inner bailey, on the highest slopes of the hill that provide the castle with its excellent position, is

French noblemen who supported the claim of John's nephew Arthur to the throne and were starved to death. By the time of the English Civil War, Corfe Castle was owned by Sir John Bankes, a staunch royalist, who withstood a protracted siege under a traitor, Colonel Pitman, admitted the parliamentarians in February 16466. The family were honorably treated by the victors, but the castle was slighted, much of the stone being used for house building in the village of Corfe.

One of the greatest castles in England was Corfe Castle, where human artifice combined with natural features to produce a fortification and residence of immense strength and grandeur. Achieving its definitive form in the reign of Henry II, Corfe Castle has an inner bailey, still with its curtain wall, and a western bailey with the remains of an early hall. The most dominant single feature is the surviving portion of the rectangular keep built at the instigation of Henry I, and the 'feel' of the site is one of total physical control of the area surrounding the castle, which was slighted in the English Civil War.

largely of 11th-century construction, with curtain walls of that period surrounding the rectangular tower keep (attributed to Henry I), a hall and other apartments, and in the south-east corner another tower. This was the core of the castle, and in the 13th century the ground plan was considerably enlarged with the construction of approximately equal sized West Bailey and Outer Bailey, the latter being increased considerably in size before the castle was completed with Edward I's outer gatehouse of 1280. The outer walls were immensely strong, and had no fewer that 10 towers along their length for additional defence; eight of these towers were placed along the south-western and southern walls, where the castle faces onto the lower sloped of the hill and is therefore most vulnerable. The castle was a favourite of John, who valued its great security as a treasury and 'home' for state prisoners: among the famous and important who suffered there were Peter of Pomfret, a hermit who dared prophesy John's downfall and was dragged to Wareham and back on a hurdle before being hanged, and 22

While Corfe was of importance principally because it commanded the south coast route west of Southampton, Dover fulfilled a similar and perhaps more important role on the south-east tip of England, guarding the port at the English end of the shortest crossing of the English Channel. That this fact was realized to be of vital strategic importance was appreciated early in England's history: the ancient Britons built an earthwork castle on the hill dominating the port, the Romans built a considerable fortification on the same site (the lighthouse is still extant within the more modern castle. Harold is believed to have thrown up earthworks in the area, and William the Conqueror built the country's most powerful castle there. Little is known of William's construction, however, apart from Peverell's Tower, which still survives. The core of the present castle was built between 1179 and 1191 during the reign of Henry II, and consisted of a towered inner bailey and tower keep. The keep was certainly the most impressive tower of its period, measuring 98 ft by 96 ft on the ground, and stretching upwards some 80 ft. The ground floor is surmounted by two other floors, and for extra structural and defensive strength the tower is divided laterally by a cross wall. The long outer wall surrounding the outer bailey is largely of 13th century construction, a French attack in 1216 revealing that the current defences would probably not have withstood a major assault supported by the siege engines that were coming increasingly to the fore. The castle was strengthened yet further on two other occasions: during the Napoleonic Wars and during World War II. These later additions detract from the historic look of the castle, but much of the oldest parts of the fortifications are still visible, including the 289-ft well in the keep, which predates any of the buildings above ground. Other notable features at Dover are the church of St Mary-in-Castra, originally an Anglo-Saxon foundation on a cruciform plan, and the extensive network of tunnels started in 1216 and extended in the Napoleonic Wars. With exists in the cliffs and in meadowland surrounding the castle, these tunnels were used profitably as late as World War II, when they served as air-raid shelters, the castle remaining a military headquarters until the 1960s.

Surviving as a viable military establishment well into the 20th century, Dover Castle shows evidence of its immensely long history in the stump of the Roman lighthouse next to the Anglo-Saxon church, the much-altered middle Norman keep (Peverell's Tower), and the towered inner and outer curtain walls dating from the time of Henry II. Further additions were made from time to time (notably during the Napoleonic Wars), these modifications including stronger gates and extensions of the outer curtain walls to the edge of Dover cliffs. The final developments are largely under the ground, and mark the castle's importance in World War II.

The function which was fulfilled for the harbour ar Dover by its immense cliff-top castle was performed farther west along the English Channel, at Portsmouth, by Portchester Castle. This is again an impressive Norman castle built on the site of an earlier Roman fortification, on a spit of land jutting out into the harbour and so surrounded on three sides by water. Before the Normans arrived, the site of the Roman fort had been filled with a defended burgh, the type of protected community much favoured by the Anglo-Saxons, especially when the fruits of earlier fortifications were available: in the same area Pevensey is a good example of this tendency, where a burgh was built on the site of Anderida fort and then overtaken by the Norman castle. The oldest part of the fortifications still surviving is the outer wall, whose Roman origins are betrayed by its rectangular shape. The outer wall and its bastions are some 20 ft high, and provided later builders with an existing outer bailey. With the burgh cleared, the Normans could then locate their own castle within the north-east corner of the 9-acre

Roman fort, the ditch surrounding the inner bailey and tower keep being probably of Anglo-Saxon origins. Responsibility for the inner bailey and lower part of the tower keep rests with Henry I, though the barbican to the former was added in the 14th century and the upper portion of the tower keep was built by Sir Robert Assheton, constable of the castle, between 1376 and 1381. In its definitive form the keep is of the sub-variant whose height is greater than either of the ground dimensions, and other fine examples of this type can be found at Corfe, Guildford, Richmond, Rochester and Castle Hedingham. At Portchester the tower is divided into a basement and three upper floors, and the same scheme is followed at Castle Hedingham in Essex, which is some 65 ft high and of oblong planform. The basement and ground floors were divided into two roughly equal portions by cross walls, that of the ground floor (or more properly entrance floor) having a gap in its eastern end. In the western corner of the tower was the circular stair that ran right up through the tower, the first floor being the great hall

surrounded by a mezzanine gallery and the second floor being compartmented into six roughly equal smaller rooms. Naturally enough, the great hall on the first floor could not have been used as such had it been divided by a cross-wall, so a massive transverse arch was used in its place. It seems that the basement was used for the storage of arms and provisions, the entrance floor as administrative and accommodation space for the lord's retainers, the first floor as a living area, and the second floor as accommodation for the lord and his immediate family. The most extreme example of the tall tower is at Norham in Northumberland, now a ruin but once a bastion of English military power in the border region with Scotland. The castle was built by the Bishop of Durham in about 1160, and its tower keep had a basement and four other floors.

Mention has been made above of the cross wall that formed a considerable portion of the tower keep's structural strength. It was also of considerable military importance, as the siege of Rochester castle in 1215 revealed. Built as the principal defence of the River Medway and its vital harbours, anchorages and building yards, Rochester castle was started soon after the Norman conquest, the builders following quite closely the lines of the Roman fortification that had stood on the spot, though the Norman edifice was considerably smaller in geographic extent that the Roman fort. However, the castle of William I's time did not survive long, the definitive castle being built by Gundulf, Bishop of Rochester for William Rufus. The walls remain, most of them in good condition, but of the rest of this vitally significant castle there is left only the splendid tower keep, which was started in about 1127. The footing of the tower is about 113 ft above the surrounding land, and the tower is basically square, measuring 70 ft by 70 ft with walls varying from 11 ft to 13 ft in thickness, adequate for strength and the insertion of spiral stair of the conventional type within the thickness of the wall, The tower had a basement and three upper floors, and was involved in three major sieges, the first being the most significant. This occurred in 1215, when the castle was invested by John. Eventually the south-eastern corner of the keep was brought down by John's miners, and the besiegers swarmed into the keep through the breach so made: the defenders, however, were able to pull back behind the cross wall of the entrance floor, which thus became the outer wall of a keep of reduced dimensions. Here the defence held out for a useful time longer before John's forces prevailed. After its capture the castle was repaired, the original rectangular cornertower being replaced by a cylindrical tower. The towers on the eastern side are also rectangular, but were added by Edward III, and the north-west bastion was the work of Richard II's reign.

Above left: Portchester Castle in Hampshire is one of the most fascinating fortifications in England, this aerial view clearly showing the basic square site of the original Roman **castellum** *with the Norman keep inserted in one corner together with its gatehouse (plus 14th-century barbican) and curtain wall. In the opposite corner of the Roman enclosure is the church of the Augustinian priory established in 1133.* **Top:** *The tower keep of Portchester dates from the end of the 12th century, and was in the 14th century covered with a slate roof, and the stone for the keep proper having been brought in from the West Country. The vertical dimension is greater than either horizontal dimension in this marvellous four-storey keep.* **Above:** *An interior view of Rochester Castle provides an excellent impression of the structure's huge strength. The castle was built, along with others, to protect the Medway River.*

One of the most impressive castles in Scotland is Tantallon, located near North Berwick on the southern side of the Firth of Forth and sited ideally to command the coastal approach to Edinburgh from the south. The castle was a stronghold of the Douglas clan, and was completed by the third quarter of the 14th century. The castle was located on a large and rocky promontory opposite the Bass Rock, meaning that only one curtain wall was required: this spanned the promontory from cliff to cliff, and had a powerful tower at each end. In the centre of the curtain wall were the gatehouse and lord's apartments, and another distinctive feature was the provision of two great halls, one for the retainers and the other for the lord. One of the most important and successful of Scottish coastal castles, Tantallon was finally besieged and captured by the English and dismantled in 1651 as part of the Cromwellian plan to weaken Scotland.

Other notable coastal castles in Scotland were Castle Sween, located on the south-east bank of Lock Sween in the Strathclyde area, Cobbie Row's Castle on the Isle of Wyre in the Orkney Islands, and Duffus in Morayshire to the north-west of Elgin. Castle Sween was the earliest Scottish castle of the Norman type, and was built in about 1220 as a large rectangular keep with massive buttresses. The castle was increased in size at later dates, but was demolished in 1647 by one of Montrose's generals, Sir Alexander MacDonald. Altogether different is Cobbie Row's Castle, built in about 1145 as probably the first stone castle in Scotland. The reason for this was probably the lack of timber in the Orkneys, and the builder, the Norseman Kolbein Hruga, thus produced a rectangular keep inside a ditch-and-bank outer fortification. Duffus castle

dates from about 1150, and was built by Freskin the Fleming for the Murray family. The original construction was a motte and bailey type, but in the 14th century extensive additions were made, the motte being surmounted by a donjon (whose weight caused the motte to collapse in part, splitting the donjon) and the bailey being enclosed with a curtain wall. The hall in the bailey was rebuilt in the 15th century, and this is still visible in the form of remains.

The greatest coastal fortification in Ireland is Carrickfergus, which was built between 1180 and 1205 by John de Coucy of his successor Hugh de Lacy. The site is a rocky spit projecting into Belfast Lough, and the castle covers the narrow spit, this wall comprising little more than a gatehouse with twin towers. It was at Carrickfergus that William III landed in Ireland on his way to the decisive Battle of the Boyne in 1690.

Left: Built on a promontory, Tantallon Castle needed a curtain wall only along the neck of the promontory for the outer defence of the residential portions of the castle position.
Above: Carrickfergus remains one of the most perfect examples of military architecture in all of Ireland.

Altogether better provided with effective coastal fortifications was Wales, the principal sites being Beaumaris, Caernarvon, Conway, Flint, Harlech and Rhuddlan, all of them in the north of the country. Beaumaris is located in the south-east corner of Anglesey, and was the last of the major castles to be started by Edward I as part of the consolidation of Wales after its capture between 1282 and 1284. The work of James of St George, Beaumaris was started as a result of the Welsh rebellion of 1294-5 and schemed as a monumental concentric castle with the multiple gateways and gatehouses that had become a feature of the English castle in the late 13th century. Such a castle was built to a markedly different pattern from the motte and bailey type that had prevailed up to about 50 years earlier, for instead of a keep located deep inside the area covered by the outer curtain walls (themselves

arranged to make the best use possible of the terrain in the immediate area), the concentric castle is based on two quite closely-located sets of essentially quadrilateral walls. In the centre is the castle proper, a massive and thickly-walled square with northern and southern gatehouses (the latter with a barbican), cylindrical towers at each corner of the construction, and semi-circular towers at the midpoints of the eastern and western walls. Outside this core lies the enclosing walls, not as tall or as thick as the inner walls, but bulged slightly outwards in plan on each face and surrounded (originally) by a wide moat. The outer enclosing wall, like the inner fortification, relied heavily on the use of flanking towers, there being three basic sizes on the enclosing walls: two large towers on the north-west and north-east corners, four intermediate-size towers on the south-west and south-east corners and along the north-north-west wall, and six small towers on the east and west walls. There were also heavily-defended northern and southern gates. There can be little doubt that Beaumaris, though never completed, was the culmination of British castle building, carefully sited (though on flat ground) and built with little regard for cost to the highest possible standards. Edward crushed the Welsh rebellion in 1296 and then turned his attentions to Scotland, work on Beaumaris being halted in 1300. Further construction was undertaken between 1306 and 1330, but the castle was never taken under siege in its original condition, its only siege coming in 1646 when it was held for Charles I against the parliamentarians until news of the fall of neighbouring Caernarvon was received.

Edward I's castles in Wales number eight, namely Aberystwyth, Builth, Flint and Rhuddlan all started

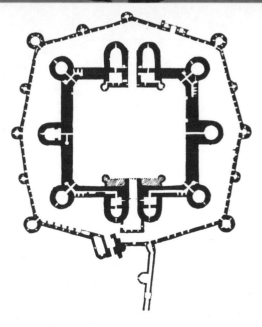

Below: Caerphilly Castle in South Wales marks one of the high points in England castle-building, being the first concentric castle of English construction. It is notable for its great size, evident power, and good water and outwork defences. *Right:* Ground plan of great Caerphilly Castle, started in 1271 by Gilbert de Clare. *Below right:* Caernavon is somewhat unusual in being linked with a walled town. It was started in 1283.

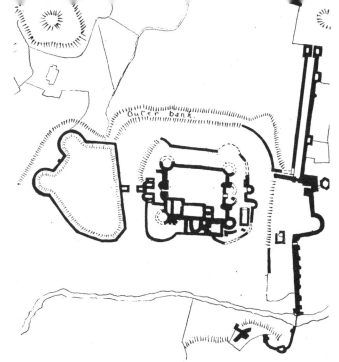

in 1277, Caernarvon, Conway and Harlech all started in 1283, and Beaumaris started in 1296. Costs varied enormously between the castles, and it is estimated that Edward I spent upwards of £80,000 on his eight masterpieces, with further expenditure following from the coffers of Edward III as he continued the work on Beaumaris and Caernarvon. Edward I's costs for Caernarvon and Conway were in the order of £27,000 and £14,000 respectively, but these two were most expensive than their brothers largely because they incorporated fortified towns within their schemes.

Massive gatehouses and enclosure walls are characteristics of Caernarvon and Conway, each of which had to conform to the rock outcroppings on which they stand, while Harlech and Rhuddlan are like Beaumaris concentric castles, though not as perfect in plan as Beaumaris as a result of the need to conform to terrain considerations.

The British isles also abound with inland castles, though again the majority are to be found in England. The castles vary enormously in size and complexity, as may well be imagined in the light of the widely differing threats, the financial situation of the builder and changing concepts of fortification.

Typical of the moderate-sized castle built in the south of England during the late 14th century is Bodiam in East Sussex. This was erected under licence from Richard II by Sir Edward Dalyngrigge to protect the surrounding area of Sussex against French marauding raids. It was the last true castle built in England, and stands in the midst of a large moat as a classically designed and sited quadrangular castle, only six years younger than the roughly similar Bolton castle in North Yorkshire, which was started under licence from Richard II in 1379. Both Bodiam and Bolton were conventional quadrangular castles surrounding an inner courtyard, a style that had become virtually universal by the 13th century despite the appearance of oddities such as Nunney in Somerset, which reverted to the old-fashioned motte-and-bailey plan, though the latter was in a sense vestigial with only limited defences.

Bodiam was entirely conventional of its type, and was built but not used against the threat of invasion during the Hundred Years War. The quadrangular keep combined both defences and accommodation for the lord and his garrison, with a large gatehouse in the northern wall and a smaller postern gatetower in the southern wall. Both structures were machicolated, that is they were surrounded at their tops by an external stone gallery to provide the defenders with superior firing positions to enfilade any attackers. Each corner of the keep is characterized by an exceptionally bold cylindrical tower, rising well above the level of the walls

Below: Bodiam Castle in East Sussex is an exceptionally fine example of the late mediaeval English rectangular castle, with first-class defensive capability thanks to its water defences and outworks. Right: Ground plan of Ludlow Castle, comprising an inner ward without a motte, and a large outer court with curtain wall.

themselves, and the two walls without gates (east and west) have strong rectangular towers in their centres. Access to the main gatehouse was protected not only by the machicolated defences of the gatehouse and the enfilading fire from the two adjacent cylindrical towers, but also by a dog-led causeway itself defended by outworks, a barbican and two drawbridges.

Bodiam was by the standards of the day an exceptionally strong castle, which lacked the sheer size of some Welsh castles but was more than adequate for the task at hand. At the same time the quadrangular keep offered many residential advantages over the tower keep, for its greater internal area allowed the usual array of great hall, chapel, kitchens, stables, stores and the like, but also

a far greater number of private rooms and suites, so providing the comfort to which the English aristocracy were becoming accustomed. The neatness of the design, however, lies in the fact that the military virtues of the castle were not sacrificed to the desire for comfort, but rather combined with it. The same tendency can be seen in Bolton castle, which nevertheless reveals a measure of its northern austerity in the retention of square towers at the corners, and the use of a simple but well-protected gate by the south-east tower. Comparable quadrangular castles were built at Sheriff Hutton in Yorkshire and Lumley in County Durham.

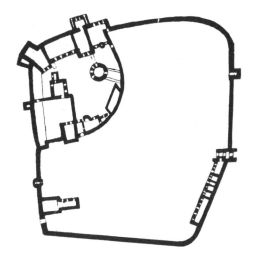

Serving a similar function in the middle reaches of the English border with Wales is Ludlow, established in the middle of the 11th century by the Lacy family from Normandy as a protection against Welsh reivers and as a jumping-off point for the inevitable English advance into central Wales. At the time of its establishment, Ludlow was merely a walled enclosure providing a modicum of protection and security despite the absence of motte or keep. Soon, however, the castle began to take on the conventional appearance of the time, with outer and inner baileys. Construction was pursued with singular vigour over a considerable period, and still extant are the late 11th century mural towers and the impressive gatehouse (the latter being converted into a tower keep during the 12th century), a particularly impressive 12th-century chapel with a round nave, and dating from the period of Mortimer occupancy in the 14th century the blocks of apartments and great hall added to the inside of the castle. And while the Mortimers were most concerned with improvements to their creature comforts, they were also responsible for the building of the massive Mortimer's Tower on the west wall of the outer courtyard. Further improvements were made in the 16th and 17th centuries, but these were concerned mostly with the administrative functions of the Council of the Marches, which was headquartered at Ludlow. As noted above, the gatehouse was upgraded to a tower keep. The gate was always of singular importance, for even the most stoutly constructed wooden gate was comparatively vulnerable in comparison with stone walls, and in the later 11th century the hitherto gated gap in the outer wall was gradually supplanted by an elaborate gatehouse which allowed the containment of any attackers who got through the main gate itself. Amongst the earliest examples of this tendency were Exeter, Ludlow and Richmond, and the substantial gatehouses of this period were then used by later generations for the development of superior vertical defences combined with extra accommodation. As an alternative to gatehouses added to existing structures, there also existed the notion of flanking towers for added protection, and such structures were provided at Dover and Worcester, the former by Henry II and the latter by John.

London, the capital of Norman England, was one of the first cities to receive a Norman fortification, a walled enclosure in the south-east corner of the city wall built by the Romans. This was built by William I in 1066, and was the basis of what is now the Tower of London, which began its approach towards its present state with the building of the White Tower, a massive tower keep within the original walled enclosure, started almost as soon as the outer walls had been completed as an initial defensive step. Thereafter progress with this most important of English castles was steady as king after king sought to improve the cornerstone of Norman rule in London. After William I's efforts, further development was made to the west, culminating in the Bell Tower erected on the orders of Richard I. Henry III was largely responsible for the inner bailey, which saw an extension of the castle's ground

Right: Undoubtedly the premier castle in England, Windsor Castle is a royal residence of long standing, and shows the efforts of builders and architects over many centuries. On the right is the Round Tower, built by Henry II, rebuilt by Edward III and heightened in Victorian times. Below: The White Tower in the Tower of London.

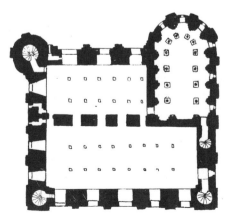

plan outside the Roman walls to the north and east. It was in the reign of Edward I that the Tower of London reached its maximum (and current) extent, with the development of the contemporary fortifications into a concentric castle plan by the addition of an outer ward with its own curtain wall, a new moat providing additional security, a water gate in St Thomas's Tower, and the strengthening of the landward defences by the addition of the Byward Tower, the Middle Tower and the Lion Tower on the southern wall; the Byward and Middle Towers still survive, but the Lion Tower has gone. Throughout this period the Tower had been the royal residence, and it was only in the reign of Henry VIII that it was abandoned in this capacity, then becoming a prison for state prisoners.

Fairly close to London is another royal castle, this time at Windsor. This is the world's largest inhabited castle, and covers an area of 13 acres on a magnificent natural defensive site close to what were once great hunting forests. The original castle, built by William I, was a modest structure on a motte, but the present fortification is the result of many monarchs' efforts, though the original layout, with a bailey on each side of the motte, is still apparent. The oldest structure still standing is the shell keep built by Henry II and rebuilt by Edward III as the Round Tower. Slightly later are the main fortifications of Henry III, notably the three round towers (drum towers) on the west wall. And later still are the state apartments of Edward III. The castle in its original form was completed by the construction of St George's Chapel, a classic of English Perpendicular architecture, in the late 15th century. Since that time most monarchs who have taken an interest in Windsor put their marks on the palace, and the whole was unfortunately 'restored' in Victorian times. As it now stands, Windsor Castle is the premier castle of England, and consists of three basic portions: the Lower Ward (including St George's Chapel), the Middle Ward (including the Round Tower), and the Upper Ward (including the State Apartments). The monarchs who made most of the later additions were Mary, Elizabeth I, Charles II, George III and George IV, for which last Sir George Wyatville developed the stunning roofline which is so much a feature of the present castle, home of the British royal family.

An inland castle farther to the north is Warwick, which enjoys with Alnwick, Arundel and Windsor the distinction of continuous occupation since its building. Unlike the other great castles of England, moreover, it fortunately escaped the attentions of Victorian 'restorers' and so preserves much of its original 'feel'. Warwick was started by William I in 1068, just two years after the Norman conquest as a fortified motte-and-bailey structure, the original stone buildings dating from late in the 12th century. However, none of the present structure can be traced back to a period before the 13th century, when the castle was the home of the Beauchamp family, the earls of Warwick. Key features of this

One of the greatest English castles, but unlike others little spoilt by 'restoration' of the Victorians, Warwick Castle has been continuously occupied since its foundation and overlooks the River Avon.

great period in Warwick's long history are the
Water Gate to the south of the motte, the many
residential buildings along the line of the river, and
(perhaps most important of all) the east-facing front
nearest the town. Here were built the most powerful
defences of the castle, including an extremely well-
defended gatehouse with barbican in the centre of
the wall, flanked to the north and south respectively
by the polygonal Guy's Tower and clover-leaf
Caesar's Tower. The wall, its gatehouse and the two
towers must be regarded as amongst the finest
examples of mediaeval military architecture in
England if not in Europe.

In Scotland the two most important inland castles are Edinburgh and Stirling. Edinburgh is the Scottish equivalent of the Tower of London and Windsor, in that it is the royal castle at the heart of the country, in this instance on a huge rock outcrop dominating the capital. The castle dates back to the 11th century, and is typical of the period despite the fact that little of this first period remains, most of the present structure dating from the 12th century with considerable later additions. Amongst the many outstanding features of the castle are the 12th-century St Margaret's Chapel. Also in the Edinburgh area is Craigmillar Castle, where there are 14th to 17th century remains. One of the most decisive moments in the castle's history came in 1567, when the Scottish nobles agreed to assassinate Darnley, husband of Mary, Queen of Scots.

Controlling the road into the Highlands lies Stirling castle, again admirably sited on a rock outcropping that gives the castle an ideal tactical position. The strategic importance of the site meant that there had been a castle there from early times, but the present structure dates principally from the 15th century, most of the important structures dating from the period between the accession of James III in 1460 and the accession of James VI in 1567. Perhaps the most impressive feature still visible are the Palace, the Great Hall, the Chapel Royal, the King's Old Buildings and the turreted gatehouse and flanking towers plus curtain wall. Other notable castles in the interior of Scotland are Kildrummy in Aberdeenshire, an enceinte castle (that is a castle with a fortified circular outer wall, like that of Queenborough in Kent) dating from the 13th century with five cylindrical mural towers but dismantled in 1715; Caerlaverock in Dumfriesshire, built to a triangular plan from the 13th century with twin gate towers at its apex and single towers at the other two corners but dismantled by the Covenanters in 1640, and Threave in

Kircudbrightshire, sited on an island in the River Dee, the castle consisting of a four-storey tower and an outer wall, all built between 1360 and 1370 but dismantled in 1640 by the Covenanters.

In the depths of Ireland there are many fine castles, perhaps the most interesting being Castletown Geoghehan, Nenagh, Roscommon, Roscrea and Trim. Located in Country Westmeath, Castletown Geoghegan is a good example of the 13th-century type of motte-and-bailey castle; located in County Tipperary, Nenagh was built late in the 12th century by the 1st Butler of Ormand, and was based on a cylindrical keep attached to the northern corner of a small five-sided ward; Roscommon, in County Roscommon, was the product in the second half of the 13th century of Robert de Ufford as a result of problems with the O'Connors, and consisted of a rectangular ward whose access was protected by a twin-tower gatehouse (Ballintubber, built slightly later by the O'Connors, was essentially similar); Roscrea in County Tipperary, was once the site of a motte-and-bailey castle, but even the motte was demolished in the time of Edward I and the present castle was built to an irregular plan with its defence centred on the gatehouse keep coming into fashion in the 13th century; and at Trim in County Meath is an impressive keep of basically rectangular shape inside a curtain wall of triangular plan and provided with mural towers including a cylindrical gate-tower.

Below, left: Stirling Castle occupies a classic position controlling access to and egress from the Scottish highlands, and has several times played a decisive role in Scottish history, a good example being the abortive Jacobite siege before the Battle of Culloden in 1746. Below: Controlling a western approach into central Ireland and the division between Upper and Lower Loughs Erne, Enniskillen was a natural tactical choice for a powerful castle.

Mountain countries such as Switzerland are ideally suited for
control by castles, as may be gauged from this view of Valeria
Castle in the Sion region.

CASTLES OF EUROPE & SCANDINAVIA

Feudalism was prevalent over most of northern Europe, though it appeared in a number of forms throughout the first four centuries of the second millenium after Christ. For this reason the feudal castle, combining protection and accommodation, is to be found in profusion over key areas of France, the Low Countries, Germany and Scandinavia.

In France, the feudal castles are massed mainly in the north of the country and along the basic line of the River Loire and its tributaries, the latter area being the site of the most impressive castles in the world, generally known as Chinon but in fact comprising a group of three castles in a row along the stone outcrop that dominates the town of Chinon in the valley of the River Vienne. The castles are arranged in an east-west line, and are separated from their neighbours by massive moats, though this factor can be little appreciated from a viewpoint in the valley below the whole agglomeration. The three castles are the Chateau de Coudray, the Chateau du Milieu and Fort St-Georges. That this was one of the earlier feudal sites is indicated by the fact that the two chateaux were started in the 10th century by the powerful counts of Blois, the work being completed after 1044, when the area passed under the control of the counts of Anjou. Largely

responsible for the completion of the two chateaux, and for the construction of Fort St-Georges, was Henry II of England, who died at Chinon in 1189. At the beginning of the 13th century the Chinon complex passed to the crown of France, which at first used the castles for the imprisonment of the Knights Templar, though the accession of the Valois line to the French throne was reflected in a gradual improvement in the amenities as an occasional royal residence. The famous Tour de l'Horloge dates from this period, and it is also worth noting that it was in the Chateau du Milieu that the young Joan of Arc had her first meeting with the French dauphin in

Chinon is in reality a complex of three castles above the River Loire, the Château du Coudray and the Château du Milieu being started in the 10th century by the counts of Blois, and complemented in the 12th century by the Fort St Georges built by Henry II of England, who died in the fortress in 1189. The whole complex was extended and integrated into a defensive unity after the area passed into French hands in 1205, becoming first a prison for the Knights Templars and then a royal residence. This important site has been maintained in excellent order up to the present.

1429, marking the revival of French capability in the second phase of the Hundred Years' War.

Farther to the north, in Normandy, lies the classic castle of Chateau-Gaillard. The castle dates from 1197-8, and was built by Richard I of England to defend his remaining possessions in Normandy and along the Seine. The castle and its fortifications occupy a lozenge-shaped plateau at Les Andelys: core of the complex is the massive keep *en bec* (that is a keep of basically circular section but elongated slightly to present a point in the direction from which it was expected the major assault would come) facing into the inner bailey. The keep and the curtain wall defences for the inner bailey are massive and high, and are surrounded by a wide ditch, in a position to command with great authority the middle bailey and its curtain wall, also defended by its own moat; finally, stretching out to the south-east is the triangular outer bailey. The whole design was intended to provide layers of defence, each line covered by that behind it. The position is an excellent one, and the design marks one of the decisive turning points in castle construction, for with it may be discerned the gradual evolution of the concentric type of castle. The castle remained in English hands for only a short time, it falling to Philip Augustus during the reign of John and heralding the English loss of Normandy. The castle was pulled down in 1603 on the express instruction

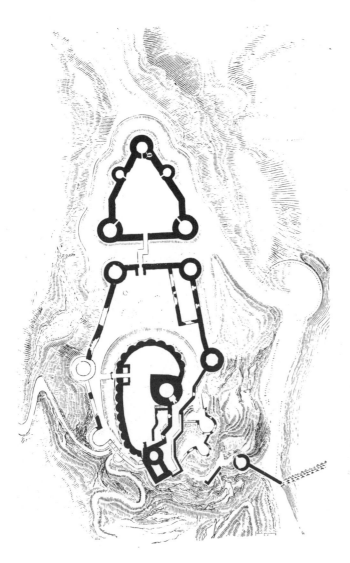

Above: Ground plan of Château-Gaillard in Normandy, one of the most impressive English castles of all time. The site at Les Andelys is a natural defensive position of great strength commanding a vital stretch of the River Seine, and on this Richard I between 1196 and 1198 built Château-Gaillard, to a design foreshadowing the English style of concentric castle. The keep **en bec** *is massively strong, and well protected by bastioned walls and a moat, with further protection afforded by outer defences and extensive ditching. Support for the outer defences could be furnished from the inner defences, providing for an integrated defence capability.*

of Henry IV of France. It seems likely that the original design complex for Chateau-Gaillard came from the smaller but comparable La Roche-Guyon built in the late 12th century to command the confluence of the Epte and Seine rivers.

Compared with Chinon, the other major royal residence in the Loire valley is markedly different. This is Amboise, and its construction in the late 15th century on the site of earlier fortifications marks the turn away from castles with the emphasis on fortifications to castles with an emphasis on comfortable residence. Amboise was the work of Charles VIII of France, who was born in the original castle and completely rebuilt the existing structure into his own palace by the time of his death in 1498.

Quite the opposite is the earlier castle at Caen, built by William of Normandy just before 1050. The site is ideal, with massive fortifications surmounting a hill overlooking the town. A huge keep was built by Henry I of England, and the castle changed hands several times in the Hundred Years' War. The end

Below: Amboise is one of the primary castles of the upper Loire, and though the present complex dates from the late 15th century, when Amboise was rebuilt by Charles VIII, the seminal importance of the site is indicated by the fact that a castle has stood here since Frankish times. Keynotes of the design are its renaissance design and great style, though closer examination reveals that military virtues have not been excluded.

for this classic castle came in 1793, when the keep at the centre of the fortification system was dismantled.

The southern half of France is not without its castles, the three most impressive of which are Montsegur, Pau and Tarascon. Montsegur and Pau are both in the foot-hills of the Pyrenees, and Tarascon commands the lower Rhone. Built in 1204, Montsegur has a five-sided plan with a square donjon in its centre, and was the last refuge of the Cathar heretics after their defeat by Simon de Montfort. Taken under siege in 1243, the great castle held out for two months, but was then taken as a result of treachery, and was pulled down as a warning to other rebels. The heretics who refused to recant, some 200 in all, were burned to death below the castle.

Located towards the western end of the Pyrenees, Pau was built in the 12th century by the viscounts of Bearn, its lofty position commanding the strategic crossing of the river below it. However, from 1370 the castle was extensively modernised by Gaston Phoebus, and considerable revisions were carried out at times right up to the middle of the 19th century.

Considerably later in basic origin is the impressive fortification at Tarascon, which rises sheer from the banks of the Rhone. The natural dominance of the site had meant that fortifications had long stood on the spot, but the current castle was started in the late 14th century by Louis II of Anjou, Count of Provence. Later modifications completely altered the look of the castle, principal

among these alterations being the raising of the curtain walls to the height of the corner towers, and the machicolation of the entire upper level of the walls and towers by King René. The castle passed into the hands of the French crown in 1481, and was much admired for its exceptionally comfortable accommodation. The castle's later history was mainly as a prison, in which capacity it remained in steady employment up to 1926.

Amongst the greatest concentration of older castles in the Loire region is Loches, an eminent site that seems to have accommodated a fortification from early times. In the feudal period the site's principal importance was as a base for the Angevins in their local power struggle with the lords of Blois. The 12th century keep raised by Fulk Nerra contains elements of an 11th century fortification, and the castle was considerably enhanced by Philip Augustus in the first quarter of the 13th century, notably by the addition of the towers *en bec*. In common with many other French castles, Loches became a prison in the period after the decline of feudalism during the second half of the 15th century. Farther to the west in the Loire area lies Saumur. It seems that the basis of the castle lies in the 10th century, but little of this original fortification can be discerned through the additions and alterations of later periods, the most important, aesthetically if not militarily, being the work of the dukes of Berry in the 14th century, when the castle was transformed into a Gothic masterpiece with considerable height, pointed roofs turrets and the paraphernalia of Gothic architectural imagery. Abandoned to the elements in the 17th century, Saumur then became a prison and barracks before being restored to its Gothic heights. Another masterpiece from the same period lies at Vincennes in the outskirts of Paris. This massive construction, with a huge keep on an older foundation and great encircling walls with nine towers, started life as a fortress on the site of a royal hunting lodge, and was begun by Philip VI. Many other French kings then took a hand in matters, and the castle was slowly transformed into a magisterial palace before becoming, in common with so many other French castles, a prison and barracks.

Left: From the landward side Tarascon castle is an imposing fortification of the late mediaeval type; but from the river side the castle it yet more impressive as its rises above the River Rhône in a way that is both morally and physically impressive. Much of the castle's current good condition can be attributed to a fair quantity of restoration work. Right: Beersel castle in Belgium dates from about 1300 in basic plan, when the circular stone base and moat were created. The current castle dates from 1491, when the three towers were built after the original fortification had been severely damaged in two successful sieges during 1489. The castle has been deserted for some centuries.

The Low Countries and Luxembourg also possess their fair share of major castles, and the three most significant are probably s'Gravensteen in Belgium, Muidersloot in The Netherlands and Vianden in Luxemburg. Located on the junction of the Lys and Lieve rivers at Ghent in Belgium stands s'Gravensteen, which was first built in the 11th century, though the only traces of this original fortification lie in the cellars of the 12th century donjon. A timber fort had stood on the site in the 10th century, and this was replaced in about 1000 by the stone donjon mentioned above. This withstood a considerable siege in 1128, but was then rebuilt in about 1180 by Philip of Alsace on his return from the crusades. The process saw the erection of the large stone donjon and other residential buildings in a bailey surrounded by an oval-plan curtain wall with 24 mighty towers, each of two storeys, the whole surrounded by a large moat. The castle enjoyed a chequered history in the 14th century: in 1301 the aldermen of Ghent were besieged in the castle by the townspeople, and forced to surrender after a fire in the castle, and in 1338 the population of Ghent forced the walls in another siege. After this crucial period the castle was widely rebuilt, the main areas of effort being the walls and the 12th century gatehouse. The castle was used infrequently by the counts of Flanders, and in 1780 was sold for use as a factory, a role maintained up to 1887.

Muidersloot is unusual amongst the castles in this chapter in being brick-built. A castle has stood on the site since about 1000, and portions of a 12th century castle are extant in the present castle, which was built in 1386 on the site of the earlier fortification, which had been destroyed in 1296. The planform of Muidersloot is square, and the castle is surrounded by a substantial moat, but in the 16th century the place fell twice: in 1508 to the duke of Gelderland and in 1586 to the earl of Leicester.

Vianden is the home of the Luxembourgeois grand ducal family, but was built during the 11th century by the counts of Vianden, passing to the dukes of Orange in the early part of the 15th century. This castle is one of the largest remaining in Europe, and most of what still stands dates from the 13th and 14th centuries. Part of the castle is in ruins, but still of considerable impact and importance are the series of gates, three in number; the large hall, which could accommodate at least 500 men, and the chapel, whose floor is pierced by an opening into a vault below.

Left: Vianden is one of the largest castles in Europe, and occupies a decisive site overlooking the valley of the River Our in Luxembourg, and is now a mixture of ruins and preserved accommodation. Below: One of the most remarkable things about the castle at Muidersloot in The Netherlands is its sturdy construction of brick rather than stone.

Farther to the east again, there are relatively fewer great castles in Denmark and southern Scandinavia. However, at Kalmar on the south-east coast of Sweden there lies an impressive fortification and residence designed to protect the region from the ravages of pirates. The origins of the castle lie in the 12th century, but the basic castle as it now stands was the work of Magnus Ladulus in the last quarter of the 13th century: Magnus revised the fortifications into a circular wall (with four round towers and two gates) with a keep in the centre. Considerable alterations were effected by Gustav Vasa, these alterations including the building of an outer rampart with great bastions for the artillery that was coming to play a decisive part in siegecraft, both defensive and offensive. In the second half of the 16th century the appearance but not the real substance of the castle was much altered to present the 'northern renaissance' look that survives to this day. In passing, it should be noted that Kalmar was one of three castles of the same basic period, all designed to combat the ravages of pagan pirates in a basically Christian area. The other two castles were at Stockholm and Borgholm. Kalmar is a castle truly steeped in history, and has been taken under siege more than 20 times as well as serving in later years as a prison, barracks and store.

On Gotland, a large island lying of the south-eastern coast of Sweden, there rests Visborg, a castle built into the corner of the walls surrounding the town of Visby. This simple but effective fortification was planned by the Teutonic Knights, but the addition to the 13th century town walls was in fact effected by King Eric during the early part of the 15th century. Eric was eventually driven out by his subjects, but was able to hold this castle in the south-western corner of the town for 10 years. Little now remains of the castle, which was largely pulled down in 1679, but the town walls are still intact, and the 2½-mile circumference is marked by 42 towers.

Much of the wealth of Denmark in the early part of the present millenium was generated by tolls levied on ships passing through the Belt, and as Denmark possessed both the southern and northern shores of this constriction up to 1658, she was well placed to collect the revenues with the aid of a fortress built on each side of the narrows: on the Danish side the castle is Kronborg at Helsingor, and on the Swedish side it is Halsingborg. Kronborg still exists in very good condition, but less is left of the massive fortification on the other shore. Here at Halsingborg only the keep is left. This was built in the 12th century, and was much improved and modernized in 1370 by Valdemar IV, who rebuilt

Above: The Kronborg at Helsingor is the Danish counterpart to Sweden's Hälsingborg, and is one of the finest renaissance castles in the Scandinavian region. There was a castle on the site as early as the 11th century, though the present palace dates from the fourth quarter of the 16th century, in the reign of Frederik II. Left: Kalmar is one of the keys to the southern coast of Sweden.

the castle in brick, its most dominant feature being a tower over 110 ft high, which permitted a close watch to be kept on the narrows for trade plying in and out of the Baltic. The castle at Helsingor is visible from the top of the tower, and this enabled boats to put out to halt any traffic. Other interesting castles in Denmark are Hammerhus on the island of Bornholm, where there remain portions of a huge castle built between the 13th and 17th centuries, originally by the bishop of Lund during a conflict with the king; Nyborg, on the island of Fyn and built as a royal palace from the 13th century onwards and largely destroyed by the Swedes in 1660; and Vordingborg, on the island of Zealand, built as a large royal palace in the 14th century over an area of 10 acres. And in Norway the most important castle is Akerhus, a combined residence and fortress of royal origins built on the orders of Haakon V at the beginning of the 14th century. Considerable alterations in the following centuries have failed to modify the original concept and layout, and the castle remains in regular use for formal functions to this day.

Typical of the castles controlling the valleys of the River Rhine and its tributaries is Burg Stalhseck, well fortified on a crag above the river and its traffic.

The location for many of Germany's greatest castles is the valley of the Rhine and those of its major tributaries, for these were the main trade routes in the west of what is now Germany. The main grouping of these castles is south of Bonn, for here the Rhine runs through a precipitous valley ideally suited to castle defences. Along the Rhine the castle concentration is heaviest between Koblenz and Heidelberg, with another concentration along the Main and the Neckar rivers.

One of the most impressive of these Rhineland castles, and typical of the appearance of this characteristically German style, is Burg Eltz on a bend of the Eltz river to the west of Koblenz where it meets the Rhine. There was a castle on the site by the 12th century, and the present castle dates in organization but not in construction from the second half of the 13th century. The castle was the home of the counts of Eltz, and this had by 1268 split into six allied but smaller branches, each of which occupied an individual *Haus* within the oval walls and surrounding a central courtyard. The castle is typical of the *Bergfried* style, with the individual tower blocks built into the curtain wall on a relatively small area, often quite heavily sloping, at the top of a natural defensive feature, in the cast of Burg Eltz a massive and isolated stone outcrop. Lower down the outcrop are the outworks of the castle, serving as a first line of defence. With the exception of the 14th century Haus Platt-Eletz in the western end of the central courtyard, the *Hauser* of Burg Eltz were built in the late 15th century, many of them incorporating where possible elements of the original structures.

Another castle surmounting a rocky crag is Drachenfels, located on the east bank of the Rhine just south of Bonn at Königswinter. The castle was started by the archbishops of Köln towards the beginning of the 12th century, and later passed to the Drachenfels family. The original 12th century castle was a massive *Bergfried*, but in the 15th century the whole castle was enlarged considerably by the addition of a curtain wall with round towers along its eastern side. The castle was abandoned during the Thirty Years' War, and the structure has slowly declined into ruin, some considerable portions of the outer works being removed in the 19th century as building material. Drachenfels may be regarded as the most northerly of the classic Rhineland castles.

Just south of Koblenz lies Gutenfels und Pfalz, a complex of two castles in widely different styles.

Viewed from the Philosopher's Walk on the other side of the River Rhine, the structure of the Schloss Heidelburg appears intact, though this massive residence-cum-castle is now no more than a partially restored relic of the seat of the Counts Palatinate of the Rhine, one of the most important ruling families in Germany.

Gutenfels is a rectangular castle, probably built by the Falkenstein knights in the first part of the 13th century, and is located on a rock promontory above the village of Kaub behind the river. The castle is made up of a large accommodation block and two wings running along the sides of the central courtyard, with a *Bergfried* at the eastern end. Outer protection is provided by a series of relatively small curtain walls each enclosing a courtyard. And below this original fortification stands the Pfalzgrafenstein, on a small island in the Rhine. The original structure on the spot was a five-sided tower, which was built in 1327 by Ludwig of Bavaria as a toll station. This tower still stands, though it is now enclosed within a six-sided enclosure built in about 1340. This outer fortification has round turrets on its corners, and was considerably strengthened at its southern end by the addition of a bastion in 1607.

Yet further up the Rhine rests Rheinfels, on a relatively low promontory dominating St Goar. This was at one time the most powerful of the Rhine castles, and its present ruinous state only hints at the size and grandeur of this decisive fortification. The original castle was built in about 1245 by the count of Katzenelnbogen as a basically square structure with one *Bergfried* tower. Considerable extensions were carried out by Wilhelm II von Katzenelnbogen in the middle of the 14th century, the most important of which were a large palace with round towers on the northern side of the site and a screen wall with end towers on the southern side of the site. In the last quarter of the 15th century Rheinfels passed to the landgraves of Hesse-Kassel, who were in turn responsible for yet further expansion and the construction of far-ranging outworks. By this period, therefore, the original castle was regarded and rebuilt as a residential complex protected by newer outworks.

The seat of the counts palatine of the Rhine was Schloss Heidelberg, seated firmly on a massive spur of rock dominating the south-east section of the city of Heidelberg. The first fortification on the site appears to have been built in about 1225, but little of this original structure remains. What remains dates from the 15th century for the most part, with additions in the early 16th and 17th centuries. As is usual with such castles, the basic plan is rectangular, with massive walls and corner towers, in this instance circular. The castle was twice captured and heavily damaged by the French in the last 20 years of the 17th century, and partial restoration was undertaken in the later part of the 19th century.

Other significant castles in Germany are numerous, but space precludes all but mention of a few of the most important. Festung Marienburg, for example, was an ecclesiastical castle, and was built on a site overlooking Wurzburg by the bishops of the area on the site of an older (iron age) fortification. The modern castle dates from about

The oldest part of the Festung Marienburg in Würzburg is the
13th-century round tower in the courtyard of the rectangular
episcopal residence of the 17th century.

1250, when a rectangular castle was built close to the beautiful Marienkirche: to this core of walls with residential accommodation were lated added a curtain wall with round towers (15th century) and bastions (17th century). The interior of the whole structure was extensively altered by Julius Echter von Mespelbrunn in the first quarter of the 17th century, and thus remodelled the castle has leaste to the present, still dominating the Main in Bavaria. Neckar-Steinach in Hessen is in actuality a group of four small castles: the Hinterburg built in the 12th century, with additions up to the 15th century; the Mittelburg raised in the 14th century; the Vorderburg tower and palace constructed in the late 13th or early 14th century; and the Schadek of which little remains but ruins in a small couryard. Veste is a massive castle just to the east of Coburg in Bavaria, which it dominates from its location on a relatively low hill. The castle is oval in shape, and consists principally of two courtyards and their surrounding buildings, the Hauptburg to the east and the Vorburg to the west. There was a castle on the site in the 12th century, but the present structure was started in the 13th century by the counts of Henneberg and continued by the dukes of Saxe-Coburg-Gotha. Little is left of the original structure other than the foundations of the *Bergfried*, and most of the present fabric dates from the early part of the 15th century, when much reconstruction had to be undertaken after a major fire. The round towers and the curtain wall on which they sit date from the 15th century, and much of the castle's present appearance is the result of 19th century restoration.

Austria has many fine castles, but perhaps the two most imnposing are Forchenstein and Festung Hohensalzburg. Forchenstein is in the very east of the country, sitting on a rocky outcopr in the foothills of the Rosalienbirge range. The first castle on the site was built at the very start of the 14th century by the counts of Mattersdorf, but from this time there has survived only the great donjon in the central courtyard. The rest of the castle is post-mediaeval, with much of the work attributable to the Esterhazy family, who took over the castle in 1622. It was this owner who recast the interior of the castle as a more comfortable residential accommodation, though defence was also bolstered by the addition of artillery defences. The fact that comfort was successfuly combined with military virtues is attested by the importance of the castle in the eventual defeat of the Turkish menace to central Europe in the 16th and 17th centuries. Even the Turks played a part in the construction of the castle, for between 1660 and 1680 Turkish prisoners dug out the well, which is a prodigious 466 ft in depth.

In north-west Austria is Festung Hohensalzburg, a castle of extraordinarily heavy appearance on the heights above Salzburg. This is a vast complex of accommodation and fortification dating over a considerable period, with little remaining of the original castle built in 1077 by the archbishop Gebhard. The plan of his Altes Schloss remains, but this extensively rebuilt in the 15th century, when the castle was enlarged but also strengthened to a great degree, the latter being achieved in part by the addition of large round towers to the curtain walls. The bastions on the outer walls were added in the

Left: Despite its later decoration, Veste in Coburg maintains its look of antiquity in its curtain wall. **Above:** *Built between 1570 and 1586, Hochosterwitz in Austria is an immensely strong hilltop castle on a site fortified as early as 960.*

16th and 17th century, but by this time the interior of the castle had reached its zenith in the hands of archbishop Leonard von Keuznatsch, who was largely responsible for the magnificent late mediaeval furnishings and decorations.

The Festung Hohensalzburg fully deserves its lofty name, as can be gauged by this view of the fortress from the Mirabell gardens in the city below.

A castle has stood at Aigle in Switzerland since the 11th
century, but the present imposing structure dates largely from
the last quarter of the 15th century, when the Bernese revised
the castle they captured in 1475. The donjon and residential
apartments are sited in one corner of a massive curtain wall
whose other three corners are marked by drum towers.

Switzerland too has its castles, reflecting the turbulence and eventual prosperity of this small country. Aigle, for example, is relatively close to Lausanne and has been the location of a castle since the 11th century. However, the present castle dates largely from the time of the Bernese occupation of the area in 1475. The conquerors occupied a castle that had been extended dramatically from its 11th century origins, but then proceeded to remodel the entire structure. The castle is basically rectangular, with the donjon in one corner and a drum tower in each of the three other corners.

Altogether different is Chillon on Lake Geneva, in which the castle rests on a small island in an ideal defensive position. The site was occupied by a fortification as earlier as the 10th century, and the current Alinge Tower and Duke's Tower date from the 10th and 11th centuries respectively. Using these existing structures as a basis for development, Pierre Mainier developed the castle enormously during the middle of the 13th century as one of Peter II of Savoy's principal fortresses. Such was the essential

strength of the position that mural towers were needed only on the side of the castle facing the shore.

Two other magnificent Swiss castles are Tarasp and Thun, the former located near the frontier with Austria south-west of Scuol, and the latter south-east of Berne. Tarasp dates back to the 11th century, and is a solidly imposing castle that is the seat of the grand dukes of Hesse-Darmstadt. Thun is a more urban castle, with a huge donjon dating from the later parts of the 12th century, when the castle was in the hands of the dukes of Zahringen, and the dominating aspect of this donjon is augmented by the large towers at each corner of this basic structure, which is surrounded by additions of a later date.

Chillon castle in Switzerland occupies a superb lakeside site on Lake Geneva. The core of the castle comprises two towers, dating from the 10th and 11th centuries, and these were built into the present structure during the middle of the 13th century, the site requiring mural towers only on the landward side of the fortifications.

Sidon on the Lebanese coast was the site of two great crusader castles. This is all that is left of the smaller sea castle, built from 1229 and abandoned in 1291.

CASTLES OF THE MEDITERRANEAN

The castle-building period in the Iberian peninsula was roughly that in which the Moors occupied much of the country; the Moors arrived in 711 and were finally ejected in 1492, leaving behind then a number of *alcazaba* garrison fortresses whose design influences were slowly melded with the tower keep type of feudal castle that was first built in the north of the region, moving slowly south as the Moors were progressively eliminated from the peninsula. Portugal is fairly evenly dotted with castles, such as Alter do Chao, Beja, Elvas, Leiris and Silves, but possibly the most important castle in the country is that at Braganza, on the north-east frontier with Spain. The present castle was built by Sancho I in 1187 on the site of an earlier fortification. The castle is typical of the northern Iberian tradition with a blocky rectangular keep of considerable height and provided with two watchtowers. The keep is surrounded by a truly formidable curtain wall of granite, the same stone having been used for the keep. Further additions were made in the 14th and 15th centuries. Braganza is somewhat unusual, for a Portuguese castle, in having its keep built into the enceinte wall; at Guimaraes, by contrast, the 10th century keep is distinct from the enceinte wall. This latter castle was built up from its earlier basis by Henry of Burgundy after his elevation to the position of count of Portugal by Alfonso VI of Castile in 1095. Guimaraes was largely rebuilt in the 15th century along current notions of geometric defence, the revised castle having a trapezoidal plan with towers in the angles. Situated to the north of Lisbon close to the coast, the castle at Leiria was built in the second quarter of the 12th century as a border fortification on the southern border of what became Portugal in 1137. The site had already seen Roman fortifications, and wherever possible these were included in the first Portuguese castle produced by Alfonso Enriques just before his elevation to the position of king of Portugal. With the conquest of territory farther to the south Leiria ceased to be a border castle, and fell into disarray before a revival in the first quarter of the 14th century, when King Dinis rebuilt the castle with a small but powerful citadel above a royal palace. The keep was surrounded by a curtain wall, and further additions were made in the late 14th and early 15th centuries.

The castle of Marvao in Portugal provides a clear indication of the layers of outer defence walls and positions to be penetrated by any attacker before he could come to grips with the massive inner defences right at the top of the position. Apart from the walls themselves, the attacker would also need to cope with the slope of the site, and the enfilading fire from the relatively few (but carefully sited) towers on the walls of this most impressive fortification, a classic of its type. The castle dates from the late 13th and early 14th centuries, when it was built as a border fortification against the ambitions of Castille.

Almost immediately after the reconquest of Segovia from the Moors in the 11th century, the Spanish began the construction of the Alcazar of Segovia right in the middle of the city, using as foundation the rocky spur that formed a natural defensive position at the confluence of the two rivers. This proved to be an exceptionally effective castle, and in the 15th century it was transmogrified into a beautiful royal palace by Juan II, who built a tower keep alongside the original keep. The Alcazar was most notable for its exquisite plasterwork that revealed the long-lasting cultural impression made on Spain by the Moors. A great fire in the middle of the 19th century did enormous damage, but much of this has since been restored.

Actually of Moorish origins are the Alhambra and Alcazaba in Granada. The Alhambra is a combined fortress and palace, and was built in the 13th century as an enceinte structure with powerful towers built into the walls. The castle is now most notable for its cool but masterly interior, a long-term decoration process completed only in 1408, and for the massive strength of the Justice Gate, built in 1348 with an entrance tunnel of vaulted construction and three right-angle corners for maximum defensive strength. Towards the other end of the ridge accommodating the Alhambra is the Alcazaba, the garrison fortress that afforded traditional protection for the Alhambra. This Alcazaba is largely of mud-brick construction and was rebuilt in the 13th century on the basis of a 9th century original structure. The basic layout of the Alcazaba is reinforced by powerful towers of square configuration. The surrender of the Alhambra and Alcazaba in 1492 finally ended the Moors' hold in Spain.

Though now in Spain, the great castle at Albuquerque was in fact of Portuguese origins, for it was built in 1354 by a son of King Dinis of Portugal to cover the approaches to central Portugal just north of Badajoz. The castle occupies a monumentally impressive hilltop site of very considerable natural strength. The town itself is enclosed by the outer ring of defensive flanking walls, and access to the hilltop enceinte fortification with a great tower and extra-mural tower is gained by a fortified passage covered by a number of other flanking walls.

Certainly one of the most impressive castles in the whole of Europe is La Mota, located on the eastern side of Valladolid. The origins of the castle are Moorish, and earlier fortification having been augmented in the 12th century to produce a massive brick-built enceinte castle, Then in the 15th century the Moors employed Christian builders to modernize the fortress, which acquired an immense bartizaned tower keep and an outer curtain wall, only a short way in front of the enceinte structure and designed for the artillery defence of the castle.

The whole castle as it still stands is the most remarkable tour de force in construction and design in brick, rivalled only by Coca near Segovia, which was built at about the same time (the middle of the 15th century) for the archbishop of Seville.

In the same general area as La Mota is Penafiel, which is built on a narrow ridge commanding the valley of the Duero river. This castle is of the type known in Spain as *gran buque* (great ship), for it is only 75 ft wide despite its length of 690 ft. Built in the later half of the 15th century, Penafiel has at its heart a massive and rectangular keep, some 110 ft high with cylindrical bartizans along its upper sides. This core is protected by an enceinte fortification whose two sides have 12 towers apiece, with another at each end and two more defending the gatehouse, which can be approached only by means of a bridge over a deep ditch.

Other classic Spanish castles are El Real de Manzanares, an extraordinary palace-castle close to Madrid in the foot-hills of the Guadarrama mountains and built in the last quarter of the 15th century; Banos de la Encina, a Moorish castle built in 967-968 by the Caliph Hakam II as the main defence of the Guadalquivir river near Jaen, and a good example of the Moorish expertise in enceinte fortifications well before the northern Europeans; and Montalban, a fine Moorish castle built on a Visigothic base close to Toledo.

Above: Coca in Spain is undoubtedly the greatest of the **mudejar** *brick castles, and was built in the middle of the 15th century for the archbishop of Seville.* **Left:** *Inside the superb Alcazar of Segovia is the monumentally impressive* **torre de homenaje**, *which was much developed by Juan II, a superb plasterwork interior being added.*

Though not a castle in the true sense of the word, the fortified city of Avila is typical of the system much favoured round the coasts of the Mediterranean, and seen in other classic examples such as Obidos, Setes, and Carcassone, which each retain a complete circumferential wall for the defence of the entire town rather than just a small portion within or just adjacent to the castle of the local lord.

Rocca Maggiore is a great castle outside Assisi, sited magnificently for natural defence.

Italy's share of castles is confined to three main areas: the northern basin of the Po river and its tributaries, the eastern and western coastal regions stretching inland up the courses of the main rivers, and Sicily. The main period of castle building in Italy was between the 10th and 13th centuries, when the previously open towns were fairly swiftly developed into fortified towns by the building of towers surrounded by plain curtain walls, the latter soon being developed in the light of experience to include enceinte towers and mural towers.

At Castello Caetani, for example, the Anibaldi family in the 13th century built a walled courtyard with a donjon, the courtyard being separated from the town of Sermoneta by a deep ditch cut straight into the rock. At the very end of the 13th century the castle was acquired by the Caetani family, who then supplemented the rectangular donjon on the southern side of the courtyard with a substantial hall. Further additions were made during the 16th century by the Borgias before the castle returned to the Caetani, who still own this fine construction.

Rocca Maggiore in Assisi is built on a ridge overlooking the town, and is one of the finest surviving Italian castles with a genuine military purpose. The site is a large area surrounded by a long curtain wall with towers in the corners, and in the angle overlooking the town is the residential block, which consists of an outer palace surrounding a courtyard containing a rectangular donjon (*mastio* in Italian). The castle was started in 1365 by Cardinal Albornoz, but was completed mainly by the *condottiere* (mercenary leader) Biordo Michelotte, who made Assisi his base in 1394. It seems likely that Michelotto completed the curtain wall and the *mastio*. Further development took place in the 15th century, when Giacomo Piccanini built a multi-sided tower to the west of the castle, linked to the enclosure wall by another wall surmounted by a covered gallery. The whole edifice was completed in 1538 with the addition of a bastion for the gatehouse.

The main fortification in Rome is the Castel Sant'Angelo, which is based on the tomb of the Roman emperor Hadrian. This tomb became a base for the internecine power struggles within Rome as early as the 6th century, the monumental nature of the tomb making it a choice location for families requiring a solid structural power base. This meant that the tomb changed hands frequently as family after family secured ephemeral supremacy in the eternal city, and it was only after the middle of the 14th century that the castle came permanently into the hands of the popes. This finally allowed modifications, and indeed enlargements, to be carried out: in the middle of the 15th century Nicholas V ordered the construction of round towers at the corners of the tomb, at the end of the century Alexander VI added to this with

Between two towers on the west wall of the Castel Nuovo in Naples is an extraordinary triumphal arch built between 1453 and 1465 for Alfonso I of Aragon.

There can be few sites more stunning and naturally strong than San Leo in the Montefeltro region of Italy, where the Rocca Feltresca has for centuries provided a magnificent refuge. Inside the walls are two churches, one dating from the 8th century and the other from the 12th century.

incorporation of polygonal towers in the basic structure, and in the third quarter of the 16th century Paul IV and Pius IV completed the present structure with a series of outer bastions.

Many of the so-called castles of Italy would be better described as palaces with a minimum of fortification, but there were also many genuine castles. These include Castelvecchio, built in the middle of the 14th century by Cangrande II della Scala to command the approaches to the Adige river in the city of Verona; Rocca Feltresca near Forli, built in the early mediaeval period in an excellent defensive position with a cliff on one side and the other protected by a strong machicolated wall; Castello dell'Imperatore built just outside Prato by Frederick II in about 1240 as a rectangular castle with square corner towers and varying towers at intermediate positions; Lucera, which is a large-area enclosure on a spur, protected by a wall across the spur to provide almost perfect protection to the huge (but now lost) tower built by Frederick II; and Castel Nuovo, an oppressive structure in Naples, which was first built for Charles of Anjou but remodelled some 150 years later in the mid-15th century for Alfonso I of Aragon.

The other main area in which feudal castles may be found is the eastern Mediterranean, all legacies of the crusading zeal of the Europeans to wrest the Holy Land from the infidel Arabs and also spread feudal ways of life into the area to alleviate the overcrowding of Europe that was becoming evident by the 13th century. There are several feudal castles on the island of Cyprus, and another clutch in and just off the southwest coast of Turkey (Bodrum on the mainland, and on the islands of Kos and Rhodes), but the main concentration in the Levant, along the coastal regions of what are today Syria, Lebanon and Israel.

The primary castle-building area in Cyprus was along the north coast, though the square three-storey donjon and surrounding curtain wall of Kolossi was built on the south coast by the Hospitallers in about 1460. Along the north coast, however, there are four main sites: from west to east these are St Hilarion, Kyrenia, Buffavento and Kantara. The castle of St Hilarion occupies an immensely strong natural position on twin mountain peaks, and the present cursader castle is built on the basis of original Byzantine fortifications adopted and adapted by the Seljuk Turks. The Turkish castle was taken by the King of Jerusalem on the orders of Richard I of England in 1191, and then handed over to Guy de Lusignan for further development during the early 13th century into a typical Norman castle with three wards, the lowest remaining must as it was when the Turks lost it, but middle and palatial upper wards being added as the real strength of the castle. The castle was much reduced in size by the Venetians later in the island's

history, but St Hilarion remains one of the most impressive castles of its type.

Kyrenia has a similar history, and was also taken by the crusaders in 1191 before being rebuilt as a Norman castle of quadrilateral basic shape surrounding a central courtyard. The castle was a centre of Lusignan security on the island, and was heavily modified later in its history by the Venetians, who after 1544 added three large bastions and thickened the southern and western walls (those facing inland) to a maximum of 130 ft as a defence against artillery.

Buffavento was also an important although lesser part of the Lusignan rule in northern Cyprus, for it formed a visual link between Kyrenia and Kantara castles and with the city of Nicosia. The site is a typical mountain one, and the 13th century castle was built on the basis of an earlier Byzantine fortification, the Norman pattern being of two wards on a natural defensive position. The position was near impregnable, but the castle was largely dismantled by the Venetians in the early 16th century as an economy measure. Much the same function was allocated to Kantara, whose natural defensive position with watchtower was strengthened in the later part of the 14th century by the addition of a massive southern wall with powerful gatehouse. Like Buffavento, the castle was demolished in about 1525 when the Venetians turned their attentions from the Genoese in Famagusta to the Turkish threat from the north.

The Levant abounds with castles, and typical of the castles taken by the crusaders and strengthened against their former owners are Edessa near Urfa in eastern Turkey, and Saone near Latakia in Syria. Edessa was already of great age when it fell to the crusaders in 1098, and the Normans immediately set about adding to the capabilities of the existing Byzantine and Armenian structure with a deep ditch cut right into the rock on which stands the castle, protected by substantial bastions. At the same time a donjon was built inside the existing rectangular walls. A similar process is evident at Saone, where the Franks in the early 12th century added a deep rock-cut ditch to an existing Byzantine fortification. Two sides of the original triangular site were protected by ravines, and the Franks completed the natural defence with their own ditch, no less that 90 ft deep. By local standards the Byzantine fortification was comparatively modern, having been built in the 10th century, but the addition of the ditch and a massive and well-stocked donjon availed the Franks little in 1188, when the castle was considerably undermanned and fell with little difficulty to Salah al-Din. Also in Syria is the well-preserved Safita, probably built by the Templars near Tartus in the early 13th century, and lost to the Moslems in 1271. There was a curtain wall for the outer defence line, but what remains today in

excellent condition is the large two-storey donjon at the summit of the round hill on which the fortification was added.

Farther to the south in Lebanon lie the remains of Beaufort, one of the most important crusader castles of the area. Built on the edge of a sheer cliff, near Arnoun in central Lebanon, Beaufort consisted of a most substantial curtain wall with donjon built into it, and was raised soon after 1120. With its eastern side protected by the cliff, the castle was made all but impregnable by storm through the provision of a ditch cut deep into the rock on its other sides. Salah al-Din took the castle in 1190 only after a one-year siege, the crusaders getting the castle back in 1240 as part of a complex diplomatic deal. Twenty years later the castle was bought by the Knights Templar, who lost Beaufort to Moslems in 1268 after a powerful artillery bombardment.

Other notable castles in the area include Chastel Pelerin, built near Haifa by the Knights Templar in 1218; Chastel Rouge, built in 1112 near Tartus as a donjon with curtain wall but lost to the Moslems in 1289; Gibelet, elevated near Jbail as a donjon with close-set curtain wall very early in the 12th century and still standing as it defied Salah al-Din's efforts at dismantling; Kerak-in-Moab, an outflung outpost in Jordan for raids on Moslem trade and pilgrims, built in 1142 near El Kerak but finally lost to the Moslems in 1188 after a savage siege; and Montfort, one of the last crusader castles to be built (in about 1230) near Naharriya in Israel, and lost to the Moslems in 1271.

But the greatest of the crusader castles of the Levant was Krak des Chevaliers, near Tall Kalakh in Syria. The site was taken over by the Hospitallers in 1142, and with it a small fortress built by the Moslems in the 11th century. A start to crusader construction was made in the middle of the 12th century with the building of a relatively small square fortification with square towers, and despite the need for periodic rebuilding after earthquakes in 1157, 1170 and 1201 the castle of Krak des Chevaliers had within 100 years been developed into the masterpiece of its time, with immensely strong and carefully considered defences: the outer curtain wall was studded with towers and extensive machicolation, while the inner bailey was further protected by towers rising from the sloping glacis of the defences proper. Access to the interior of the castle could be gained only through a covered passage that was also heavily defended. The castle never fell to a Moslem siege, but finally capitulated in 1271 when it was cut off from any chance of relief.

Krak des Chevaliers in Syria marks the apogee of the crusaders' castle-building expertise, and was developed on the basis of an earlier Arab castle as an immensely powerful concentric fortification. The small inner castle, of rectangular shape, has only one point of access, and is surrounded by an inner bailey of immense strength, with drum towers rising out of a masonry talus and so virtually impossible to scale. This inner bailey is itself protected by a substantial curtain wall, with regularly spaced towers and a machicolated outer gallery.

We should particularly like to thank the various Tourist Boards and other organisations who helped with illustrations for this book.

For reasons of space alone some of the credits have been abbreviated as follows:

British Tourist Authority - BTA
Department of the Environment, London - DofE
English Tourist Board - ETB
French Government Tourist Office - FGT
Military Archive & Research Services - MARS
Scottish Tourist Board - STB
Swiss National Tourist Office - SNTO
Wales Tourist Board - WTB

Front cover: Spanish Tourist Board. p1: FNTO. p2.3: WTB. 4-5: Sheridan Photo-Library. 6-7: Northern Ireland Tourist Board. 9: DofE. 10: WTB. 10-11: ETB. 13: BTA. 15 ETB. 16-21: DofE. 22-23: STB. 23: Northern Ireland Tourist Board. 24-26: WTB. 27: WTB. 28-29: MARS. 30-31: DofE. 32-33: ETB. 35: Northern Ireland Tourist Board. 36-37: SNTO. 38-42: French Government Tourist Office. 43: Netherlands National Tourist Office. 44: Luxembourg National Tourist Office. 45: Netherlands National Tourist Office. 46: Swedish Tourist Board. 47: Danish Tourist Board. 48-49: Lufthansa. 50: Verkehrsverein Heidelberg. 52-53: Tourist Information Würtzburg. 54-55: Fremdenverkehrsverband Franken. 55-57: Austrian National Tourist Office. 58-61: SNTO. 62-63: Sheridan Photo-Library. 64-65: Portuguese Tourist Office. 66-69: Spanish National Tourist Office. 70-75: Italian State Tourist Office. 76-77: Cyprus Tourism Organisation. 78-79: Sheridan Photo-Library. 80: STB. Back cover: Belgian National Tourist Office.